PERFORMANCE ON DEMAND

How to Gamify Your Life to Win in Everything

PERFORMANCE ON DEMAND

How to Gamify Your Life to Win in Everything

By Seth Humphrey

Performance on Demand

How to Gamify Your Life to Win in Everything

ISBN: 9798690531485

Cover design by Sooraj Mathew

Edited by Hilary Jastram

▮▮▮BOOKMARK

DEDICATION

I dedicate this book to my father, Charles "Sonny" Humphrey. I'm using your life as my purpose to lead others from a life of regret.

RESOURCES

Head to momentumactivator.com to get started on your 30-day coaching trial to kickstart your momentum today!

TABLE OF CONTENTS

INTRODUCTION viii

DISCOVERY 16

    CHAPTER 1 THE WORLD OF FRANCHISES 18

    CHAPTER 2 THINKING DIFFERENTLY 24

    CHAPTER 3: ANOTHER LEVEL, ANOTHER DEVIL .. 30

    CHAPTER 4: STEPS TO STEPPING OUT 38

    CHAPTER 5: BREAKING THE CYCLE 44

    CHAPTER 6: THE GORILLA ALLIANCE 50

SELF-MASTERY 64

    CHAPTER 7: FORECASTING 66

    CHAPTER 8: OWNING IT 76

    CHAPTER 9: THE FIX 94

    CHAPTER 10: THE VITAL 4 FOUNDATION 100

FOCUS, AIM, EXECUTE 120

    CHAPTER 11: CLEARING HURDLES 122

    CHAPTER 12: CHANGE YOUR STORY 134

    CHAPTER 13: CREATING UNBREAKABLE
    COMMITMENT 140

    CHAPTER 14: FUEL FOR CHANGE 146

    CHAPTER 15: MOTIVATION MEANS ACTION 152

    CHAPTER 16: PERFORMANCE IN PLAY 166

ACKNOWLEDGMENTS 172

ABOUT THE AUTHOR 173

INTRODUCTION

<u>This is not your normal self-help book.</u>

I'm not your normal coach. This book is filled with how-to actionable steps. I'd read so much about setting goals, routine, working out, and nutrition that I found myself overwhelmed with possibilities. No book I have found yet has laid out the "why" you would undertake making these changes in your life and matched a simple structure to follow, so that's what I plan to do.

I value simplicity and try to keep every area of my life simple.

Most gurus out there want to sound smart, so they blab on using fancy terms, trying to keep you confused.

If you stay confused, then you'll always need the guru. This was the problem I had with some coaches I've used in the past. They'd give you just enough that you couldn't pass them up, but then they left you wanting more, aka you would have to spend more to keep the coach.

This denial of knowledge feeds into a scarcity mindset, and this rubbed off on me early in my business relationships. It took me realizing one very important factor to get away from it.

Want to know what I realized?

I realized that the more I give, the more that comes my way in the form of meaningful relationships and business success.

And so, I'm giving it all to you today...if you keep reading.

But first, I want to explain some of the struggles I've been through because I believe our challenges prepare us for something larger that we'll be prepared for.

The last four years have been a whirlwind of obstacles, from losing my father, to almost losing my business twice, to losing individuals who I cared greatly for.

Through all of the resistance, I broke the code on how to get results.

Not just in your health or how you look, but in every area of your life.

My program helped my college friend and online client Nate Nelson drop over 135lbs. in under a year. I'll tell you more about how we did that later.

It helped a 44-year-old man in England working in internet marketing become a commercial pilot.

It has helped a lot of men gain control of their emotions and improve themselves, which led them to get married (call me Cupid).

In this book, I'm giving you the exact same program that produced these results so you can experience the results that you want to live the life you dream of.

It's simple—but it's not easy. And it is worth it.

Before I tapped into what worked for me, I thought that I was different, but I soon realized we're all the same.

I thought I was a little bit crazy.

That no one understood the stuff I was going through.

So, I kept to myself for a long time.

But once I shared my story, I realized I was not alone.

"Pain shared is pain divided."

Other people are struggling like I was. Just like you might be.

You want your life to be different. You know that you're leaving a lot on the table, and that's a sure way to have regret later.

If you follow my system consistently, you can experience the changes my clients have. Better yet, your world will change.

But be warned: with growth comes resistance.

As you move forward and take the initial steps, you will inevitably be tested to see how bad you really want it.

In saying that, I'm going to show you how to deal with the inevitable resistance that will be thrown at you. You will know not only what you need to do to get ahead, but I will give you the formula that works to stay ahead. So, you won't lose your gains when you come up against the resistance.

I'm excited to share with you what has saved not only my life but hundreds more.

I look at life as a game, and in the end, I want to know I went all out playing to win.

The problem I see with most people is that they're playing the game, but they're not keeping score to know if they're winning.

Think about it, if Michael Jordan played a game all-out in the NBA finals and put it all on the line to win, but when the game ended, he found out that no one kept score, all his hard work would come down to guessing whether he'd won.

This is how most people live their life. We want to be great fathers, spouses, business owners, and men who live with a purpose.

Yet, most only know if they're winning or not by either what their bank account reads (it'll never be enough FYI) or by what the scale reads.

There is no point system that tells us we're being great husbands or fathers.

That's where I struggled for so long because the only way I could tell if I was winning at life was by comparing myself to others.

So, what's the answer then?

We need to gamify life.

We need to work toward a goal at all times.

We need to know if we're winning or not. That's exactly what I'm going to do in this book: show you how to make life a game.

Too many of us base our results off how we *feel*. I hear this from my clients all the time: "I *feel* like I'm getting better." Whenever I hear the two words, "I feel," I know that we're playing a game in la-la land, which is fantasy.

The truth is that we need facts to move closer to the results we desire.

Life is a lot more fun to play when we're dialed in rather than wandering around just feeling like we're winning.

Your mind is the happiest when it's making progress, and most don't know if they're progressing or not.

So, it's no wonder so many high performing individuals deal with suicide and depression because they FEEL (there's that word again) like all their hard work is leading to nowhere.

Then what's the point, right?

We only get one shot at this game called life. I've made it my purpose to lead men away from a life filled with regret, and you'll find out why as we move forward.

I look forward to taking you on this journey; buckle up.

-Seth Humphrey

P.S. I've created a 30-Day Momentum Activator to help high performing men FEEL better. How we feel impacts every area of our life. If you don't feel good, you won't go the extra mile in business or your relationships. If you don't feel good, you won't have the energy to work out or play with your kids. I'd love to invite you in for thirty days to work on creating the momentum to keep moving forward. I hear a lot of people say they need motivation, but in my humble (and 100 percent accurate) opinion, you must create the momentum to jumpstart the motivation. I'd love to show you my simple program that will optimize how you feel on another level. Just click the link to join here: momentumactivator.com.

DISCOVERY

CHAPTER 1
THE WORLD OF FRANCHISES

"It doesn't get easier; you just get stronger."
-Unknown

It's crazy to think how one decision can open up your world to so many possibilities.

That's exactly what I experienced when I received an innocent email from my franchise Strongarm United.

Strongarm United was a one-on-one personal training franchise, and the email told me they were planning to add to their business model.

Soon small group personal training would be a service we could offer.

Strongarm United called this small group personal training "PACK."

To get this new venture off the ground, Strongarm United put on a challenge.

The challenge was to get the franchise owners to take one of their one-on-one rooms or studios and transform it into a small group room.

Whoever could transform their studio or room best would win the challenge.

"I'm the type of guy that if I'm going to do something, I'm going all in."

I got to work.

It just so happened that a mattress store a few doors down had closed. That left a 3,200 sq. ft. spot wide open.

Seeing an opportunity to upgrade, I requested taking a look inside. I tell you all this because it's a key part of the story. It illustrates how badly I wanted to win that challenge.

Once I decided to take the leap, I signed a new lease for the larger location, even though I'd just renewed my smaller location months earlier.

In my mind, this was going to be the move that made the franchise recognize me.

Up until that point, I had received little-to-no recognition for the numbers I'd put up in a small town in Oklahoma.

This expansion would show corp that I was not messing around.

Since I was moving and expanding, it was the perfect time to open another business that would fit nicely with my personal training studio.

So, right next door to Strongarm United in the place where the mattress store had been, I installed a business called StretchU.

With my focus entirely on these two businesses, I neglected even doing the simple stuff that keeps me on an even keel.

I know better, but I fell off the wagon anyway, and my anxiety skyrocketed.

I quit working out, eating right, and investing in myself.

I was on autopilot and possessed to complete these tasks. I couldn't fail.

So, I put my head down, got to work, and the team, and I did it. Both doors opened in November of 2011.

At one point, I had pushed myself so hard that as I sat in the doctor's office, I told him: "I just feel like I'm always having a heart attack."

The doctor looked at me and asked, "How much have you been working out and doing the stuff that you usually do to manage your anxiety?"

I told him I didn't have time to do what I normally did. I was under two extreme deadlines.

He told me to go back to working out and sent me home with some anxiety medicine.

That was a crazy time in my life, and as I sit here, I realize how much that talk with the doctor impacted my life. You'll find that out later.

Even while feeling like I was having a perpetual heart attack, we had completed the opening of both businesses.

The mattress store had been successfully transformed into the new and improved Strongarm United, and I had added StretchU as well.

I invested over $35,000 to make it happen.

When we reached the finish line, it was time for my recognition. I just knew I was winning the contest.

Strongarm United was going to announce the winners at our annual conference in St. Petersburg, Florida.

I remember thinking, *there's no way I won't win this award!*

CHAPTER 2
THINKING DIFFERENTLY

"Challenges are what make life interesting.
Overcoming them is what makes life meaningful."
-Joshua J. Marine

Some lady from Missouri walked away with the award and vacation. I wasn't sure where she was going on vacation because I didn't stick around long enough to find out.

I couldn't believe how wrong I had been.

I was pissed, especially when I found out the changes she'd made. They weren't nearly as elaborate as what I'd done.

All she did was take one big room in her facility and install a plastic-like shade thing that she could slide across a track that ran the length of the room to make two rooms.

I had invested $35,000 and moved from a 1,200 sq. ft. location to a 3,200 sq. ft. location. Not to mention, I had dealt with all the logistical headaches involved.

To say I was pissed was an understatement. But I can now see that the lady went above and beyond to deliver value to the franchise.

I, on the other hand, created enemies so I could perform. I made everyone my competition, and if you didn't sing my praise, you were against me.

Looking back, no wonder they chose her. I also realize as I grow older, that life isn't fair.

Just before I left that event in St. Petersburg in 2012, I sat in a conference room and wrote myself a letter. Then snail-mailed it to my gym in Yukon, Oklahoma.

Around three or four days later, I opened that letter and read it:

"Dude, you've been disrespected. You have been overlooked, and when you get back, you're going to work. You'll never be overlooked again."

And right when my feet hit the floor in Oklahoma, I was back to work with a chip on my shoulder.

Thankfully, I got rid of that chip.

That started me on a path of thinking differently. I had to admit to myself that I didn't know everything. I knew I had to seek out other people for help.

So, I found individuals who were where I wanted to be, and I followed their lead.

One guy I followed talked about meditation, specifically Holosync, on CD.

That was enough for me. I got the CDs and listened to them for an hour and a half every morning.

In truth, I actually slept through many of them because I was waking up at 3:00 AM to try to get everything done. My to-do list was stacked. I was paying extra attention and care to my share of the businesses.

At the same time, I was taking the doctor's advice and investing in my fitness every morning.

I spent a lot of time starting to work on myself. I was on the last path I would take to become unforgettable. I was bound to make a big enough impact that people would never forget what I had done to grow these businesses.

Little did I know that the impact of earning recognition by building big businesses would be the hardest wall I ever hit.

But I kept on despite the challenges.

In June 2013, I upped the ante and hired a couple of coaches. This was a huge investment in myself. The cost was $1,000 a month.

But it turned out this was the right decision to make. These coaches transformed my business and took it to another level. I can't give them all the credit, of course.

I still had to put the work in to level up. I still had to show up every day and keep my commitment to myself.

But it was way easier to do with a $1,000 bill auto-debited monthly.

"That investment gave me the leverage to take massive action."

Soon, the business was growing like crazy.

And my plans for the business seemed just as crazy sometimes.

I started 2014 with the big, lofty goal of growing my business forty-three percent.

It was already a successful business, but I said to myself, *you know what? I'm going to show these guys what I'm made of and what I can do for this business... Forty-three percent growth would put me at half a million. That's going to make me happy. There's no way that won't make me happy.*

I really thought that *this time* I had figured out the magic formula to being happy and creating what was missing in my life.

Well, again, I was wrong.

Throughout 2014 I did exactly what I had done in the past, put my head down, accepted no excuses, and got to work.

At the end of 2014, I had done exactly what I said I was going to do. I hit my goal of $500,000 in business.

"I had finally hit the money mark and received the praise that I thought would make me happy."

The only problem was that I had more anxiety and stress, and I had more clients that I didn't really dig working with.

So there I was, thinking the praise was what I needed to be happy. When that didn't work, it had to be the money.

It was like I'd climbed all the way up the ladder of success, but the only problem was it was propped up against the wrong house.

CHAPTER 3
ANOTHER LEVEL, ANOTHER DEVIL

"You don't become enormously successful without encountering and overcoming a number of extremely challenging problems."
-Mark Victor Hansen

Fueled by my unhappiness and wondering why I was so unfulfilled, I turned to my coaches. At that time, I had seen a change in them. They had started investing in and focusing on all of the other areas of their lives. They lasered in on their family, took care of themselves, and did not party as much. I noticed they were simply becoming better individuals all the way around.

In November of 2014, they invited me to an event they were hosting. I jumped on it and signed up immediately. They gave me simple habits to put in play daily, leading up to the event in January. They mixed these habits with some in-your-face accountability that helped me gain clarity and shot my confidence and energy through the roof.

The crazy thing is I was going through this event with seven other men, and none of us knew what to expect.

In January 2015, in San Diego, I met up with these men to catch a quick bite before the event started the next day.

To tell you I was scared doesn't describe how I felt. These men and I speculated over what we thought these coaches might have us do. We were trying to read the future, which was just causing our fear to rise. Regardless of our coaches' plans, we had already invested time and money, so there was no backing out for me.

We broke away for the night with strict instructions to meet at 5:00 AM at an address near Pacific beach.

The four days we spent together were a whirlwind of emotions. It was the realest I'd ever been—

especially in front of other men. But I was as clear as I'd ever been at the same time. It was almost as if when I dropped the mask I'd been wearing that I felt free for the first time. What I realized was that I'm not as crazy as I thought I was. All the stories and my self-bashing were exactly what the other men at the event felt as well. But since no one wanted to be the crazy one, we suppressed our feelings and emotions.

My biggest takeaway from the event was how big of a hypocrite I was. I also learned if you give a man money who doesn't have the vital areas of his life in order, a disaster is waiting to happen.

After I finished the event, I was sitting in the San Diego airport, texting all my loved ones to show them know how much I appreciated them. It was about 6:00 AM Pacific Time, which made it eight o'clock in Oklahoma.

My sister texted me back and informed me that after 30-plus years, my mom and dad were separating.

This was a huge shock.

I couldn't help thinking: *right after this eye-opening event, I get hit with this news?*

It was then that I realized I was headed down the same path as my father. The experience in the airport made me feel like I'd gotten slapped upside the head. That's when I knew: *Dude, this is why you're here. You didn't just go to this event for the heck of it.*

You went because you have something you need to learn.

I want you to take note of the timing of this news and then write down this nugget of knowledge.

"When you decide to level up in life, the obstacles will come."

These obstacles serve an important purpose.

They present themselves to see how badly you really want that next level.

At that point, I realized I had a decision to make.

I could go back home and use the tools my coaches had given me to take action.

Or I could go back to what I had always done in the past and get the same results.

I just couldn't do that to myself or my family again.

I looked at my dad, who had kicked the can regarding his health because he insisted on putting his finances at the forefront of everything.

He put business first, thinking that by showing up financially for his family, he was showing his love.

He didn't take care of himself and didn't take care of his relationships. Ball games and important events were attended by other family members, but rarely him.

He never took vacations with my mom and the family.

All because of business.

There's no doubt he was a trooper. He had survived several heart attacks and had lost his mom when he was just seventeen. On the day she died, he was supposed to drive her somewhere, but for whatever reason, he didn't. She had a seizure behind the wheel and passed away in a car wreck on Christmas Eve.

He never spoke about it to anyone.

On Superbowl Sunday in 2007, he couldn't get ahold of my uncle Mike, so he kicked in the door to find his little brother, his business partner, and his best friend who lived on the same acreage we lived on just down from our pasture, dead of a heart attack.

My dad never discussed it.

I saw the ways that my father had messed up and realized that he was just doing his best.

He was doing what he had been taught by his father—not showing emotion and suppressing his feelings. My dad, like many others, chose alcohol and food to sedate his emotions.

It was all becoming so clear to me that my dad had done his best. After all, no one shows us how to deal with stress and resistance.

I became aware of all the judgments I'd ever made on people, clients, and especially my son. There were directions I needed to take to fix that.

I told people what they needed to do.

I'd tell my son:

"You need to eat better."

"Athletes eat this way."

"You don't eat like that if you're an athlete."

Then, as soon as he turned his head, I would shove all the stuff I told him not to eat down my throat.

Yes, I was a hypocrite, but I was determined to change.

"Our judgments are a compass to self-improvement and I wanted to be my most elite version."

So I became hyperaware of my judgments, which was exciting for me! Now, I had a map to follow to start working on myself.

The only problem, as I said earlier, is when you decide that you're ready to make a change, the obstacles and resistance are on the way.

Now that I understand this, when I look back on the hundreds of individuals that I've coached over the last fifteen years, the number one thing that I saw happen EVERY time was when one decides they are going to level up, problems almost immediately pop up.

After hitting those big numbers in 2014 and then going through that big transformation in January 2015, I started working on myself on a whole different level.

Understand, as I said before, when I do anything, I do it BIG.

I focused on myself and the self-development side of my life like crazy.

I invested $30,000 a year on even <u>more</u> coaching to push me. If someone has what I want, I'll pay to get in front of the line.

A few months later, in May of 2015, I went back to the Strongarm United conference and won the awards that I had wanted for so long. I finally got the recognition I'd hoped for.

Shortly after I won those awards, I realized it wasn't Strongarm United that I needed the recognition from.

I needed to recognize myself and the power that I had all along.

CHAPTER 4
STEPS TO STEPPING OUT

"Your comfort zone is nothing but a belief. A mere reflection of your thoughts. You desire something better, yet you fear change.
Self-doubt will bind you there. Belief is all you need." -Isaac Marano

Still seeking more fulfillment, I decided that my ten years with Strongarm United had been great, and I had learned so much being a franchise. But it was time for me to part ways and start my own journey.

In June 2015, my contract ended, and I told Strongarm United I was done.

"Unfortunately, I was young, dumb, and didn't do my research."

When I'd signed a new lease a few months earlier, another year had been added to it, and I'd never realized it.

I should have read the lease thoroughly and paid attention.

Strongarm United told me, "Okay, it's been a great ten years, but you have to move your business eight miles away to do any kind of personal training."

How was I going to do that when I had to honor my lease for another year?

My franchise had been my livelihood for the past decade, now all of a sudden, I had no backup plan. Strongarm United wasn't budging on what they wanted me to do.

I had no choice but to fight back.

I didn't back down.

I told them, "I'm not going anywhere."

And I didn't.

Instead, I changed the name of my business and painted the walls. I did everything I could do except leave the location.

Strongarm United then hired secret shoppers to get pictures of me doing business. I didn't have the mental capacity to deal with it all. *I had built a successful business for ten years; now, all of a sudden, my business could be taken from me?*

I remember one day around noon when I was sitting at home, and my wife called me after she got off the phone with the lawyer.

The lawyer had told her that at any time, the franchise could put in an injunction and shut me down.

All the pressure of not being able to run my business caved when the lawyer's fees came in left and right.

I remember lying down in the middle of my living room floor, almost in tears after getting off the phone with my wife.

"It was at that moment I said a prayer asking God to please bail me out of the situation."

It wasn't five minutes later that I received a call from my buddy from college, Ryan. I usually don't answer when I'm busy or dealing with something, but for some reason, I answered his call.

We made small talk for about five minutes before Ryan finally got to the point of why he was calling.

"Man, I meant to call you a couple weeks ago," he said. "But I just got busy. I feel like God put something on my heart to tell you. You're going to go through some tough times, and I'm not saying it'll be easy, but what I will tell you is that on the other side, you're going to be blessed on another level. It may take a while, but just keep pushing."

Wow! I still get goosebumps telling that story. I know it sounds out there, but that's the God's honest truth.

That call has been a constant reminder of what I already knew and what Ryan knew, too. The resistance was just beginning.

After putting me through a bunch of hell, Strongarm United gave me an option to sign back with them for a year to get me through my lease. It was my best option, and I rejoined them.

Also, at that time, another Strongarm United franchise in Oklahoma called me because they were about to go through the same obstacle with the Strongarm United corporation. Their contract was ending, but they weren't going to move.

I gave them my advice and went on about my day.

It wasn't but a few months later that I realized I hadn't seen the other franchise owners on my social media.

Sure, enough, they had unfriended me when they rebranded from Strongarm United and stayed in the same location.

Strongarm United took no action on them like they did me. This will be a big part of the story moving forward, so stay tuned.

CHAPTER 5

BREAKING THE CYCLE

"The earlier you intervene, the better chance you have of breaking the cycle."
-Don Strassberg

I'd gone through some crazy stuff, but I anticipated that my life was going to slow back down. I was looking forward to what this new peace would bring. Maybe I could finally get my thoughts straight.

But then the next obstacle showed up in April 2016.

My father became ill with sepsis. His feet were swollen huge. Since he had heart disease, sometimes he couldn't feel his feet due to the lack of circulation.

When he developed a sore on the bottom of his foot, it turned to sepsis, which is a poisoning of the blood.

At this point in his life, his heart had already weathered a few heart attacks and was really weak.

My dad fought for three months.

In and out of the hospital.

By July 19th, 2016, my father had been in the hospital for months. Doctors struggled to keep fluids off him. The doctors were going to try one last procedure, and my dad was so hopeful that this would be the procedure that worked.

I'll never forget that day.

The doctor walked in, and my dad perked up, waiting for the news. But then the doctor turned directly to my sister and me and asked that we speak in the hallway.

"When we stepped out, the doctor informed us there was nothing else they could do."

My dad was retaining fluid. They couldn't give him any fluids because they couldn't get any out.

He was drowning.

After this bombshell news, my sister and I stepped back into Dad's room. She went straight for a chair when my dad asked, "What'd he say?"

I had to look my father in his big blue eyes and let him know there was nothing else the doctors could do for him.

The regret dimmed in my father's eyes.

All the kicking-the-can on taking care of himself, not taking vacations with the family, the lack of investment in his relationships, and where else in his life he had fallen short, it was all there on his face.

All that he wanted to accomplish, that he told himself he would accomplish, never would be.

I saw the realization dawning on his face: *this is it*.

That's when I had a realization myself. Nothing teaches us how to deal with stress. Nothing teaches us how to balance everything that life offers.

The event that I went to in 2015 changed my life and gave me the exact strategies, habits, and tools to learn and practice exactly that.

"I could have a four-dimensional life."

I could be fit and healthy.

I could deal with stress and the emotions that dictate my decisions.

I could invest in the relationships I truly cared about.

Using what I had learned, I knew I had the capability of taking my issues and turning them into positives and valuable lessons.

I could learn how to take my judgments of others and realize that they were actually judgments of myself.

Everything that I needed to do to not have the same regret my father did, I now had the tools for. My life could be different.

"I didn't need to die with heartbreaking regret."

When I left Dad's hospital room, I knew that my purpose in life was to take my father's story and turn his life into a lesson.

I knew I had to use his name to help others find the change they were seeking. I had to help them make sure they made the decisions they needed to, so they didn't have dying regrets.

What I'm going to share with you are exactly those steps.

They're simple, so they won't overwhelm you.

They're laid out for you and will change the game for you...but you have to put them into play.

Since you're reading this book, I know you want to upgrade your life like me. You want to take it to the next level. So...keep reading.

CHAPTER 6

THE GORILLA ALLIANCE

"Don't wait for extraordinary opportunities. Seize common occasions and make them great. Weak men wait for opportunities; strong men make them." -Orison Sweet Marden

After losing my father, I went to work to suppress my emotions. I knew that if I had the problem my father used to, then more men would also have the same issue.

I'm a coach, so when I learn something that changes my life, I feel it is my moral obligation to share.

My coaches had pushed me to start my own program to help motivated men who need a sounding board as well as some competition.

Having other men who are pushing themselves like me and who can hold me accountable at the same time as themselves was powerful. It was time to share what I'd learned.

I often wonder how different my father's life would've been if he had opened up and shared what he was feeling.

If there is one thing you take from this book, I hope it is this, pain shared is pain divided. I know I said this before, but it bears repeating. We often keep our problems or obstacles to ourselves. When we do this, it's like putting your hands over your eyes. There is no clarity.

But you're a smart dude, and you know what you need to do. You know your issues better than anyone, so please understand that when you open up and talk about your problem, you move from covering your eyes to seeing a balcony level view.

> "What I mean is that you can view your problems from an aerial view. When you do, you often can solve your own problems."

It was time to start the Gorilla Alliance. It would be made up of a group of powerful men striving to reach their most elite level in every area of life. The goal would be to become a four-dimensional man in Fitness, Faith, Family, and Finances.

The Gorilla Alliance became my new obsession, and it took off right away. I had six months left on my Strongarm United contract before I could move three miles away from the franchise location to start a brand-new venture.

I knew that I wanted to buy a building, and my staff was all-in with excitement, too. It was time to take things to the next level like always.

We looked for buildings in Yukon to buy that were outside the 3-mile radius and found that options were very limited.

I wanted to do a little more research about the other franchise owners who had stayed in their same location. So, I did some snooping, and sure enough, they were still personal training in the same space where they'd operated their Strongarm United branch.

At that time, I started looking at all my options. I learned of a gym that was about a quarter of a mile from my Strongarm United. The owner had been trying to sell it for years. He had hit me up in the past to see if I had interest, but I didn't at the time because it was a big 10,000 sq. ft. gym, and I just did personal training in small groups and one-on-one coaching.

By then, I was becoming pretty desperate, and I knew the building owner was in the same boat, so we started to talk.

My plan was to add more businesses to the building and make it a one-stop-shop for health and fitness.

I had sold my previous business, StretchU, to my manager, and he was ready to sell back.

So, my plan was to have my personal training and StretchU operational. We would help individuals with their mobility and flexibility. It went right along with my personal training.

I also had an employee who wanted to start a meal prep place inside the building as well. This venture was starting to become super exciting!

In Yukon, the local high school is called the Millers, so I named my business The Vitality Mill and decided to buy the building.

I was so thrilled with everything happening, so I shared on social media what we were about to launch in January of 2017.

The next thing I knew, I was contacted by my franchise. They asked me about The Vitality Mill and had noticed I was breaking the three-mile radius.

My first thought was *screw them! They're going to come at me again, but they've let other franchises off the hook that didn't even move locations.*

There was no way I was going to let this fly. I had dropped well over half a million dollars on a new building.

I denied that The Vitality Mill was a gym and told Strongarm United that it was a commercial property investment, and others were paying me rent to lease space.

The franchise wasn't buying it, but there wasn't much they could do but try and get proof of what they suspected.

I had a brand-new rebranded business and more expenses coming in, but I couldn't market my business like I needed to. Or, that was *the story that I bought into.*

You'd think the franchise letting others stay but treating me differently would be an issue, but it wasn't.

Let me add clarify something else before I explain what I mean.

When I bought my franchise in 2006, there were nineteen franchises in Oklahoma. But all of those franchises had closed with the exception of two in Jenks, Oklahoma—and they were a two-hour drive from me.

I thought that once my lawyer understood Strongarm United wasn't holding other franchises to the same rules, it'd be over.

I had to hire a lawyer out of Colorado because that was where the corporate headquarters for the franchise was.

Turns out, the lawyer I hired had lost a similar case in the past. We had a lot on the line, and if we fought, the lawyer let us know that the franchise would drag out the case to try to break us. If we wanted to go that route, we should be ready to drop anywhere from $150-300k in lawyer fees.

"I fell into a dark place."

I had busted my ass for eleven years to build my business, and now there was so much going against me.

The franchise was also secret shopping us. I had to hide anyone who came in as a potential client and then interrogate them before signing them up.

One thing that stayed constant during this dark time was that I woke up and practiced all the habits I had learned in the past. Without my morning routine, I would've been in an even worse place.

The legal stuff regarding the franchise wasn't going anywhere, but life had to go on, so I leaned heavily on my faith. Again, I had everything I needed to get through this hard time.

A few months before I lost my father, I had built a spiritual relationship with a guy who became my coach for six months.

Having the faith to wake up and control what I could control and not worry about what was happening down the road was huge for me.

This is a skill that more people need these days, and I'm going to give it to you in this book.

I was battling the lawsuit and losing money left and right. I was depressed, and it felt like I had no creativity or clarity. It was like a wet blanket had been thrown over me, and I couldn't find my way out.

I was in a super dark place, but I was making it. Then one weekend, my wife and son went out of town, and I stayed behind.

I was out with a client grabbing a bite to eat when I received a text from one of the coaches who had helped me so much and who had taught me to practice the habits I spoke about earlier.

He was hitting me up to let me know my payment didn't go through. The message was straight to the point, and the way he phrased it hit me hard.

I was struggling, but instead of checking in about how I was doing, my coach became very aggressive about a payment that didn't go through.

I'd spent so much money with this dude and had so much respect for him that the way he addressed the payment really messed with me. Looking back, I was in victim mode but couldn't see it at the time. My whole life was out of control, and I was always blaming other things or people for not getting their shit right. There were always obstacles to why I couldn't accomplish my goals instead of finding different ways to get around the obstacles. Still, I felt like he should have checked in with me and shown that he cared for me more than he cared for money. This situation influenced me to change my coaching. I now push myself to be better and check in on my clients more often, so I always know what's going on with them.

I went back to The Vitality Mill that Saturday and sat in the dark, wondering how the hell I was going to get out of the spot I was in. It felt like everything and everyone was stacked against me.

I had some scary thoughts go through my head at that time. I thought about just ending it all.

Then I immediately flipped my focus to my son and wife. Thank God I didn't do anything stupid. I just kept reminding myself *you have everything you need*.

As the year went on, the franchise lawyer applied pressure but never took action; I'm guessing because the corp knew that me leasing a building wasn't against the contract.

This loophole kept them from taking action, and I kept plugging away in my ventures.

Then one day in November 2017, I decided to drop into a local coffee shop to warm up.

I never went to that coffee shop. But as I walked in, I spotted my spiritual coach, Steve, sitting in the corner.

I ordered my coffee and sat down for a quick chat to see how he'd been doing.

We chatted for a minute, and then he asked me about the franchise issues and how it had been going.

I told him that the HQs were still reaching out and threatening but never taking action.

"That's when Steve said something to me that I took as a sign from God."

"The Seth I know doesn't let things like this stop him and would've taken action on this a long time ago."

He was right; I would've fought, but my lawyer was scared.

I left that meeting and immediately fired my lawyer. I then looked for the best franchise lawyer in Colorado, but Strongarm United already had them.

So, we found the second-best, and ironically, they had succeeded against Strongarm united in the past.

We laid it out for Strongarm United: "Here are our new lawyers. If you're going to do something, then do it. If not, then leave us alone."

I never heard from Strongarm United again after that.

As smart people, we make things way harder than they have to be.

I've learned that the hard way.

I've been the fat guy.

I've struggled with gambling.

I've struggled with sedation tactics, whether drugs, alcohol, or some other substance.

I've been there.

My mission is to take these strategies and tools I've learned that have changed my life for the best—and share them with everyone.

I do this with my clients inside the Vitality Mill.

But I also do this inside my online men's coaching group called the Gorilla Alliance.

As a coach, when I learn something, I coach it and share it with others. That takes my learning to another level.

The biggest thing that I want you to take from this first chapter is that your obstacles are coming.

There's no way around it, that's what life is. Especially as you level up!

Life is all about struggles and obstacles.

The difference between us and the others is that we want to be the best that we can possibly be.

That's why we're here, after all.

Let me ask you: if we know the obstacles are coming, wouldn't it be smart for us to be prepared for them?

That's what I'm offering you...the tools to unlock energy, confidence, and power to stand firm and battle the obstacles that are coming.

These ten strategies that I'm going to lay out for you in the second half of this book are just the beginning.

I want you to use them to build the foundation to establish a routine and put healthy habits in place that will change the game for you.

This isn't theory. I'm living what I'm teaching you. I've seen these exact ten steps change my coaching clients' lives in the areas where they've needed it the most, too.

SELF-MASTERY

CHAPTER 7
FORECASTING

"The best way to predict the future is to create it."
-Peter Drucker

We all want to be our best version.

The problem is we lie.

We lie about how we feel.

We lie about our results.

We lie about what we truly want.

And since we lie, there is no clarity.

Not having the clarity of where we're going makes it hard to stay the course.

What's the 30-Day Momentum Activator?

That's why in my 30-Day Momentum Activator course, we get clear on the reality of our current circumstances; this gives us a well-defined starting point.

From there, we implement simple habits and hacks to help us produce more energy.

Why energy?

A majority of people use the excuse that the reason they don't do this or that is because they don't have the time.

What I've found is we don't have a time issue; we have an *energy* issue.

When we don't have energy, we don't go the extra steps.

When we don't have energy, we're usually in a negative mindset and low mood.

When we don't have energy, we don't show up in the bedroom or go on date nights like we'd like to.

When we don't have energy, we don't go out and play with our kids.

When we don't have energy, we don't go above and beyond in business.

When we don't have energy, we don't show up anywhere in our lives.

My program is designed in phases; the first phase calls us to do everything we can do to start making us feel good from the start of the day.

Why?

Because when we feel good, it impacts every area of our lives, so that's the main focus of the first thirty days.

The first thirty days are meant to get your mind and body firing on all cylinders. Then you feel good, and you've gained some confidence, but more importantly, you have created lots of momentum.

Not only that, you're taking data and watching your momentum build daily. Like I've said before, your mind is happy when it's working toward something.

When I was in a depressed state in 2017, I wasn't tracking or working toward anything because I was too busy trying to predict the future.

That is why it's vital that you're always working toward something, but you also need something larger than yourself to believe in during your journey.

I've wasted a lot of time in life not getting clear on what I truly wanted, which led me to climb the ladder and get to the top only to discover it was leaning against the wrong damn building.

I don't want that for you, so at the end of this chapter, I've included an exercise you can put into play.

The first thing we want to do before we get started is to "Forecast" where we're going. This is about the only time I'll tell you to look into the future; usually, I will want you to concentrate on the here and now.

I want to give you some insight on how doing this helped me because I believe you'll be more likely to take action.

"Let me tell you a story about how I know Forecasting works."

Forecasting Your Life

In 2015, I was at a mastermind with the same coaches I mentioned earlier, but this event was just for fitness business owners.

My coach asked us to make a mark on a piece of paper and then envision where we'd like to be in three years.

I wrote down that I wanted to own a building and put all my businesses under one roof. I wanted this building to make people's lives healthier, but in a simple way—it would be a one-stop-shop for health and fitness.

Then I added staff and clients who loved being a part of our family.

Fast forward three years, and I was sitting in my office inside The Vitality Mill one day, going through a box of stuff that needed to be put away.

In the box was a notebook that I didn't recognize. Being curious about what I might find in the notebook, I opened it up.

That's where I found the drawing of everything I had plotted out three years prior when I was working with those coaches.

I was blown away because I was *sitting inside* the building that I talked about—The Vitality Mill—that housed all four of my businesses.

This is a true story. It is a testament to the power of Forecasting your life.

Forecast the Vital 4 Areas of Your Life

In the first step of this process, I want you to get clear on what it is that you want.

I know this can be a tough exercise, so let me make it easier on you.

Say we're sitting here a year from today. Ask yourself what has to happen for you to be happy with your results? This is where the Vital 4 areas of your life come into play. Let me explain.

To go forward into meeting your greatest goals in life, you need to make sure that you are taking care of specific areas that will allow this.

The Vital 4 areas are Fitness Faith, Family and Finances.

Now that you know this, I want you to answer the question of what has to happen to you to be happy with your results in the Vital 4 areas.

I'll give you some ideas by going over my targets with you.

When I see myself a year from now in the Fitness category, I envision myself weighing 200lbs. I'm lean, confident, mobile and flexible. Anything you throw at me physically, I can do whether it's running, lifting weights, or doing yoga.

If I look at my Faith side, I want to be a leader in my church. So, what has to happen for me to be a leader in my church?

I know I need to take a few classes so the church can find out how I can best serve. I want to attend church weekly with my family. I also want to tithe weekly to show my faith.

Inside my marriage, I want to have a closer relationship with my wife. To do this, I need to step up and listen to what she needs from me, but I also need to set times for weekly date nights.

The more time you spend on being specific on what has to happen and on getting clear on what that will look like, the easier it'll be to break down the steps.

Once we know where we want to be in a year, we can break down what needs to happen in each quarter, each week, and then each day.

When there is no clarity, it's impossible to come up with a game plan. That's why it's imperative that you take the time you need to get specific. Otherwise, you will just waste time and energy bouncing around from one goal to another.

Action Taking Time

Take out a notebook, turn to a fresh piece of paper, and write this down.

"Fitness - In one year, in order for me to be happy with my results in fitness, I need to…"

Remember, the more specific you can get, the better.

I'm going to take you through this exercise step by step in each of the Vital 4 areas, so it's imperative that you stop now and take the time to get clear.

If you don't do it now, then you probably won't do it later because you'll be overwhelmed with all the value I'm about to give you.

So, do yourself a favor and block off some time to get clear on what you really want in the Vital 4 areas.

In the next chapter, we will find your obstacles and the solutions to fix those obstacles—which will later be your goals/targets.

Don't move forward until this is done.

CHAPTER 8
OWNING IT

"Making mistakes is better than faking perfections." -Unknown

Until we are honest with ourselves, we'll struggle to get the results we truly desire.

I believe that every change starts with our body because it's the vehicle that gets us to where we want to go.

Each client I work with goes through my 30-Day Momentum Activator program, where we focus on our behavior, and fitness and nutrition.

We do this because we can always look to improve and learn new habits that will lead to behaviors that will pay big dividends down the road.

"Putting the focus on your health is the quickest way to restore power, confidence and energy."

But there is nothing more important than how we feel. It impacts everything we do on a daily basis.

How you show up as a parent.

How you show up as a business owner, employee, or friend, and the list goes on and on.

As we're focusing only on the Fitness side, now, I'm going to ask you to rate your Fitness on a scale from 1-10.

Ten being the very best version of health and fitness you can envision.

One being the worse.

Where do you fall in this range right now?

<u>Fitness</u>

Let's break up Fitness into three categories and rate each.

The first category in Fitness is our Strength.

How strong are you from 1-10?

Next, do the same thing for your Cardio, one being you can't walk around the block, and ten is based off what you believe a ten looks like. The cool thing about rating ourselves is that the ratings come down to your perspective.

What's one look like to you?

What's a 10 to you now?

What I love is that as you progress, the rating scale will progress.

"In this comparison with yourself, it's a race to become your best version."

The last category in Fitness is Energy. So, where are your energy and overall state?

Are you tired all the time?

Rate yourself from 1-10 in all three areas of Fitness.

Once you have a number to start on, you can get clear on what will fill the gap from the number where you ranked yourself to the number 10.

You might be lacking in accountability, having a plan/program, getting more sleep, needing to quit snacking after dinner, etc.

I'm going to help you gain more clarity through these exercises later on, but that's the first task I need you to focus on right now.

All we're doing in this moment is just getting to the facts.

Of course, you will do that for every area of your Vital 4, but gaining control over your health makes everything else fall into place. It makes reaching goals in the other areas easier to reach.

A lot of the time, we talk about how great of shape we used to be in back in our high school years.

That's over with.

Right here, right now, is all that matters.

Once you're clear about what fills the gap, you should have a list of obstacles to work through.

Now let's take a deeper look at our Faith.

Faith

Faith pertains to my relationship with God. You'll do the same thing here as you did before—rate yourself from 1-10 and see where you need to improve.

It could be attending church on a more regular basis.

It might be increasing your offering or teaching a class.

It could be that you need to invite more people to church.

I'm also going to rate my Clarity in Faith, meaning how present I am in this area. Lastly, I will rate how well I handle Stress/Pressure.

Go ahead, on a scale of 1-10, rate your Relationship with Faith in your life, or God or whatever you choose. In my humble but 100 percent accurate opinion, I believe we need to have faith in something bigger than ourselves.

Next, move on to ranking yourself from a 1-10 on Clarity.

Meaning, how clear are you being with yourself on what you actually want in life?

Do you know what you need to do?

Do you need coaches or help?

Are you clear on what your purpose is and what you're here to accomplish?

When I lost my dad and realized the similarities in the problems we dealt with, I found my purpose.

I linked a horrible situation like losing my dad and flipped it to where I could use his story to help more men.

That is now my purpose is to lead men away from regret, and a big part of this mission is this book.

I'm asking you these questions because once we identify the problems, we can switch the focus on how to fix them.

The last question for Faith is: how well do you handle Stress and Pressure?

Are you anxious because you're trying to read the future?

Do you lose your cool at the end of the day?

I had a major issue with not controlling my actions on the weekend. To take on the stress, I sabotaged my health and bank account.

I gambled to take my mind off stress until I couldn't tolerate losing any more money, then I quit and found another sedation.

The same went for food. It was like a new Seth checked in about noon on Friday. All my actions weren't aligned with what I wanted in real life. I would eat as much as I could get my hands on, which led to me wake up tired, overwhelmed and frustrated on Monday.

I didn't start to change until I became aware of the time I was wasting. I wasn't willing to tolerate that.

We'll start to identify how to increase our capacity for stress as we go deeper into the book, but for now, let's return to the exercise.

Family

Follow the same process for Family that you did for Fitness and Faith.

Where do you rank as a husband or partner?

Where do you rank as a parent?

Where does your sex life rank?

Most will gloss over and tell themselves that they're good, or they'll blame others.

How do I know?

Because I was that guy, and it didn't change until I understood that everything is my responsibility.

Look at the word "responsibility" when we break it down. It means the "ability to respond." It doesn't mean you're right or wrong; it refers to what is yours to manage.

In everything we deal with, we have to respond one way or the other. We always have a choice. It doesn't mention anything about perfection, so don't go there in your mind. Don't get defensive. Just answer the questions honestly.

Knowing that no one is perfect is very exciting to me because it means we have a choice.

It's kind of like those choose-your-own-adventure books I had when I was a kid. I'd get to a chapter and have a decision to make. Would I open the door and move to chapter five, or would I go through the gate to another destination?

What I learned was that you never know about the adventure, but you're guaranteed to learn lessons and grow as you embark on it.

I also learned that you can't have courage without fear, so you might as well take the leap.

You're almost done. One more category to go.

Finances

Go ahead and rate yourself in your Finances from 1-10 just like you did before.

You will rate your Finances in two ways.

The Freedom to do what you want when you want financially and how you measure up in profitability.

I can already hear it: "Seth, I don't own my own business."

Well, then rate yourself on your Happiness with your current level of income from 1-10.

When you do this, you can see how you can add more income. On the flip side, if you hit a ceiling, it might be time for a change or a talk about how to change so your finances will improve.

What I love about Finances is that in playing the game of expansion, when you hit a 10, the ranking starts over again.

I'm going to throw one more "F" into the equation: Fun.

Fun

Rate your answers to the following questions based on the 1-10 scale again.

What's your ability to have non-destructive fun?

I find that most of us have no clue how to have fun unless it centers around food, alcohol, golf, hunting, work, or some other substance

Now hunting and golfing aren't bad, but most of the men I know who do both drink when they golf.

Or they spend so much time on the hobby that it becomes destructive because if you're like me, you will go way overboard on the stuff you like.

You might spend so much time in what you love that you lose focus on the other areas.

So, for Fun, I want you to take in to account two areas.

Rate yourself on the Experiences you're making from 1-10.

Are you going on vacations?

Are you going on date nights?

Are you hanging with friends?

Next, rate yourself on your recovery based on a scale of 1-10.

How often are you getting massages?

Are you taking time to treat yourself with cryotherapy or float tank experiences? Are you paying someone to stretch you, or maybe do some yoga?

It could be that you haven't been hunting or golfing in a while and need to add that back into your routine.

Now, understand that with every positive, there is a negative.

With every drawback, there is a benefit.

The men I know push hard, but when I ask what they do for non-destructive fun, they look at me like I'm crazy.

Understand this; if you're pushing hard and not backing off, you will redline. When you do, you'll waste more time and energy than if you'd just allowed yourself to back off.

We have to change the way we look at our Fun and let it work *for* us instead of against us.

Action Taking Time

Now let's take out another blank piece of paper and list your Vital 4 areas.

Fitness

Strength 1-10

Number you scored:

Once you identify your number, then list what will fill the gap from the number you ranked yourself at to the number 10.

I.e., "I need to strength train, work on body weight movements, hire a coach to get a program written, etc."

List out as much as you can think of to fill the gap, then identify in numerical order which task is the most important.

For example, if I've never strength trained, then I need to focus on mastering bodyweight movements first.

What fills the gap from the number you scored to 10?

Cardio 1-10

Repeat the same steps above.

Number you scored:

What fills the gap from the number you scored to 10?

Energy/Overall State 1-10

Number you scored:

What fills the gap from the number you scored to 10?

<u>**Faith**</u>

Repeat the same steps above.

Relationship with God or your Faith from1-10?

Number you scored:

What fills the gap from the number you scored to 10?

Clarity 1-10?

Number you scored:

What fills the gap from the number you scored to 10?

Present 1-10?

Number you scored:

What fills the gap from the number you scored to 10?

Stress/Pressure Capacity 1-10?

Number you scored:

What fills the gap from the number you scored to 10?

<u>Family</u>

Repeat the same steps above.

Relationship with Spouse/partner 1-10?

Number you scored:

What fills the gap from the number you scored to 10?

Relationship with Kids 1-10?

Number you scored:

What fills the gap from the number you scored to 10?

Sex life 1-10?

Number you scored:

What fills the gap from the number you scored to 10?

Finances

Repeat the same steps above.

Freedom 1-10?

Number you scored:

What fills the gap from the number you scored to 10?

Profitability 1-10?

Number you scored:

What fills the gap from the number you scored to 10?

Bonus...FUN!

Experience 1-10:

What fills the gap from the number you scored to 10?

Recovery 1-10:

What fills the gap from the number you scored to 10?

CHAPTER 9
THE FIX

"The only way out is through." -Robert Frost

Our next focus is what we need to Fix.

We want to know what the problem is because for us to change, we have to be aware.

"Awareness always precedes change."

Ask yourself: what are you knowingly doing that is stopping you from the results you desire?

This is a question that makes most people squirm, but you still need to answer it and stick to the facts.

What are you knowingly doing right now that's stopping you from getting the results you want in your Fitness and in your Fuel?

We're focusing on Fitness and fuel right now because I want you to gain power over yourself.

You're trying to regain momentum and have more confidence, focus, and clarity.

You're trying to fix the problem that you have right now before you can move on and fix something else.

It's like having a car but not getting the oil changed or the fluids filled and then wondering why it's breaking down.

You need to fix the problems in Fitness and Fuel to perform at your best.

Your answer to this question is going to help you.

It will help you get clear on what you're doing and what's holding you back.

"When you're clear, you're aware."

Then, and only then, can you start building the habits that you need to be empowered and successful

After you answer these questions, the good news is that you're at the beginning of fixing the problem that has been plaguing you.

Then you can start putting a focus on the solution to the problem daily.

Action Taking Time

On a blank piece of paper, Write down the Vital 4 areas. Under each, write out as many self-inflicted obstacles that you're knowingly creating for yourself. I'll write a few examples under each to get you started.

Remember that once you're aware, then you can change. So, be honest with yourself and take some time filling this out before you move forward.

Can you relate to these examples? Do they inspire you to share your own?

Fitness

- Late-night snacking

- Eating too many cheat meals
- Drinking too much at night, causing you not to wake up and attack the day.

<u>Faith</u>

- The Faith experience is different for everyone, so I am going to stray from the bullet point formatting. I'd study the Bible daily but not go to church, for example. When people would bring up church, I would think: *I'm doing more than the majority who attend church*. Then I had a client invite me to his church, and that's when I found the right church family. It changed my perspective.
- Everyone will be different.
- Remember, Faith is about Clarity, Focus, and how you handle stress as well.

<u>Family</u>

- On the phone too much.
- No date nights.
- Low energy causing you not to play with your kids.

Finances

- Overthinking
- No systems
- No marketing
- No clarity on the purpose
- Waiting for the right time

CHAPTER 10

THE VITAL 4 FOUNDATION

"The loftier the building, the deeper must the foundation be laid." -Thomas A. Kempis

"Foundation" is the next step.

It is a subject with many layers, and there is a lot to dive into that we will build upon, so this chapter will be a little longer.

This Foundation is called The Vital 4. I have spoken of it many times. It feeds into everything you are doing, but it also so critical too who you want to be that it deserves its own chapter.

The Vital 4 is broken down into the four "F"s: Fitness, Faith, Family, and Finances.

My friends, there is nothing more important than how you feel. That's at the base of your foundation.

"If you don't feel good, you won't take action on what's required."

You won't have the confidence.

You won't have the certainty.

You won't have the focus.

You won't have the energy.

If you don't feel good, you're only going to do the minimum or what's required.

You won't show up for your family on the level that you could if you were feeling well and energized.

You won't show up for your coworkers, staff, or friends, and most importantly, you won't show up for yourself.

We have to feel good.

That's the most important thing.

That's also why I don't want you to leave your house without completing your Vital 4.

We have a saying in all my coaching groups, "Hit your Vital 4 before you hit the door."

Now, don't get me wrong, there will be days that you have to leave your house and have to finish some of the Vital 4 later. That's okay. Exceptions will happen, but just make sure that you're trying your best to get as much accomplished as you can before the day kicks off.

This brings me to the four zones.

The Four Zones

- Zone one is: 6:00 AM to 8:00 AM.
  That's the ideal time to hit your Vital 4.
  If you can hit it in between those times, you're on the path to a great day.
- Zone two is between 8:00 AM to 10:00 AM.
- Zone three is 10:00 to Noon.
- Zone four is The Danger Zone. That means you have waited too long to do anything and have let someone else control your day for you.

When you put off the Vital 4 and reach the Danger Zone, you are telling me that you don't want power over your day until the afternoon, evening, or even night!

That's far too long to wait. Your control of your day will get away from you and will be harder to reel in, leaving others in control.

I want to have power, and I want to feel good before I talk to my wife and son.

I want to be on top of my game before I talk to clients and deal with what's going on at work. I need to be on point before I face anyone or anything that requires my full attention.

When I take care of myself first, it enables me to walk in with ultimate power, so when obstacles get thrown at me (and believe me, tests ARE coming), I'm handling them in power because I've taken care of and deposited into myself first.

> **"I can solve these obstacles and deflect them from impacting my day because I am so strong and centered."**

It is much harder and far more tiring to wait to step into your power and then use the little that's available to get through life's hurdles.

"A reminder, The Vital 4 is broken down into the four "F"s: Fitness, Faith, Family, and Finances. So remember this as you read ahead."

In addition to the questions you answered earlier in these 4 areas, every day, you can also earn 4 points within each area, adding up to a total possible score of 28 points by the week's end.

It is vital to keep score because this is a measure of success. Knowing we are succeeding gives us fuel to keep going and the proof that we are moving forward.

I've seen it first-hand.

My clients that hit 24+ points each week fly. They get great results; the momentum keeps them going.

The individuals who score lower than that struggle. And they will typically keep struggling until they prioritize their Vital 4. That's why I want you to hit it so hard in the morning.

Here's how you score your Vital 4.

Fitness

In Fitness, you receive half a point for breaking a sweat.

Breaking a sweat might be taking a 30-minute brisk walk. It may be going to the gym, doing yoga, or stretching at home. It could be doing a number of different activities.

I've created something for my clients called "The Vital Lift," which is a mini mobility/flexibility workout that leaves them in the right state of mind. (Email me at Seth@TheGorillaAlliance.com with the subject line "Vital Lift," and I'll send it to you.)

Fitness is only 10-15 minutes of you taking a little time to get your blood pumping.

When we do this, we have more certainty and confidence. We feel the best that we possibly can. Endorphins go through the roof when we break a sweat in the morning.

Let me be clear this doesn't have to be a full-blown workout; you can do that later in the day. We want to get the *benefits* of a workout first thing in the morning, so don't overthink this.

Breaking a sweat = .5

Your next half a point comes from having a green shake.

Green shakes are pretty simple.

Email me at Seth@TheGorillaAlliance.com, and I'll send you my favorite green shake recipes.

Simply put, it's just throwing in some frozen kale or spinach in your blender, a liquid base (almond milk, coconut milk, water), and frozen berries into a blender, and away you go. If you want to add in some protein, go for it. If you want to throw in some fats, go for it—then you'll have a full meal, aka protein, fat and carbs.

Some people go to Tropical Smoothie or their local smoothie shop. That's fine, but if you do this, stay away from added sugar or turbinado ("A partially refined sugar that retains some of the original molasses, giving it a subtle caramel flavor.

It's made from sugarcane—a non-genetically modified crop…")[1]

I've started my day with a green smoothie for so long now that I want to make it fast. I want to make it easy, but I also want to get the most nutrients possible in that shake.

I use a green powder that is mixed in water. Then I shake it up and go.

So, to recap…

Fuel = drink a green shake every morning =.5 point

Fitness (combining Fuel) = .5 break a sweat + .5 drink a green shake = 1 point

Once you have accomplished what you need to do in the Fitness portion of the Vital 4, you can move on to the next area: Faith.

Faith

When it comes to Faith, since we're always moving forward, and going, going, going in our lives, it is easy to understand why Faith can slip from our sights.

1) https://www.healthline.com/nutrition/turbinado-sugar

But we have to have Faith that things are going to work out and that we're doing what needs to be done.

What I mean by this is that I urge you to quit worrying about what's going to happen down the road.

We have to have faith in ourselves.

Your first half-point in the Faith area comes when you write down three wins that happened the day prior.

When you do this every morning, it shifts your focus to winning. We all know that what you focus on is what you get.

"Where focus goes, energy flows, and results show."

And these are not just clever sayings; they are true. If you want to focus on having a great day, tell yourself you are going to pay attention to everything that is making your day great. *Boom, great day!*

If you focus on all the stuff that you didn't get done, then that's where your mind will be for the whole day. *How you are always behind. How you could always do more, and that when it comes to living, you are not living up to yourself.* What a terrible self-fulfilling prophecy!

When you write down 3 wins from the day prior = .5 point

The next half a point that you can earn in Faith is meditation.

Simply put, take the time to be alone and silent to quiet your mind.

You can accomplish this in a manner of different ways. You could follow a guided meditation app. You could turn off the lights and sounds in a room and create a quiet atmosphere. Then as you sit there, breathe in and out through your nose.

Maybe you want to invest in a quick little nap to supercharge your energy?

You could go for a walk in the morning to break a sweat and combine the first part of Fitness with the last part of Faith. Just make sure to leave your phone and all other distractions at home. It should be just you and your thoughts as you are quiet and walking.

You might want to turn the radio off in your vehicle, so it is silent on your way to work.

The goal is to achieve 20 total minutes of meditation/quiet time throughout the day. Give your mind a chance to process! Even if it takes you multiple meditation sessions to get there, that is okay.

Your day should definitely start with 5-10 minutes of quiet in the morning. From there, get in the remainder of the 20 minutes before you walk in the door to see your family in the evenings.

Meditation makes us not so reactive. It makes us pause before using short-term emotions to make long-term decisions (never a productive idea!).

"We live our lives very reactively."

If somebody cuts us off in traffic, we immediately flip them off.

When we take the time to meditate, we create space so that we have a clearer mind to make decisions that aren't so reactive, and that might impact us poorly.

Instead, we make decisions based on *what we actually want*.

How powerful is that?

You can take a little time to back off of the busyness of your world to make decisions that you won't regret when you lay your head down at night. Doesn't that make taking the time worth it?

You and I both know the answer to that question.

What I see with a lot of individuals who don't meditate in the morning (or at all) is that they might kill it on their nutrition for breakfast and lunch. But when the evening rolls around, they're tired, stressed, and have been thinking all day without giving their mind a break. This has a negative impact on them understandably.

Then they start becoming reactive.

They make decisions based on what's available and based on the little bit of reasoning ability they have left in their minds.

They might grab food they don't even want, but that makes them feel good in the moment. They don't want to think beyond that or do any work because their mental reserves are so low.

Then their whole day of making sure they eat healthily is shot.

This is why we use these measuring sticks in the Vital 4—to maintain control of what we can to the best of our ability.

Faith = .5 point for writing out your three wins + .5 point for meditation = 1 point

Now you have one point for Fitness and one point for Faith.

It's time to move on to the next area of the Vital 4: "Family."

Family

To earn your first half a point, send a video, text message, note, or whatever it may be to your significant other letting them know how much you love them. Let them know how grateful you are for them and what you appreciate about them.

It's as simple as that.

Appreciation text to significant other = .5 point

For your next half a point, you need to send a text, note, or whatever to another important person in your life.

This text might go to the person on the other side of a broken relationship. It might go to your kids, mom, dad, siblings, clients, friends, or whomever you choose that day.

Family = .5 point for the message to your significant other + .5 point to text one other person of your choice.

The last point of your day will come from your Finances.

Finances

Do not overthink this part.

We all have an area of genius that we want to improve.

When it comes to my Finances, I'm going to study something in marketing, sales, culture or whatever it may be to improve my business financially.

You're also going to take 5-10 minutes to study, read a book, listen to an audiobook, watch a YouTube video, or do whatever else you can think of to make you or your business better financially.

While reading, when you find a tool or tip that you can implement, something that gives you an idea, write that down and save it for later when you will put it into play.

Whatever it may be, you need to study and execute on it. This can impact your finances.

Finances = .5 point for studying + .5 point for executing.

*****

Chad Yearwood is a great client and friend of mine who worked with me for years.

He was in insurance and wasn't happy with what he was doing. He had pushed hard and worked his way up the corporate ladder, and then he was not happy anymore.

I told him, "You're not happy with what you're doing. Why don't you find something else?"

But he was so caught up with the retirement that was coming at the end of his career that he wasn't ready to make a change.

Then, one day he finally listened to me.

He started working on the side to get certifications and qualifications in another line of work. But he had to do it in his spare time, studying in the morning on topics that didn't pertain to his career.

Ultimately, he found a job he enjoyed much more once he earned those certifications.

He now works in a career that pays him more money. And what he studied he could put into his new business.

Then he had two things going for him, which opened him up to many more opportunities.

"There are reasons we do what we do. We want to get better. We want to improve."

These small investments that we are talking about making daily will make real changes to our lives.

That is what the Vital 4 will do for you when you work it to your best ability every single day.

But also remember that every single day you need to keep score.

Because how will you know you're winning if you're not keeping score? You need that reinforcement. You need to look at your numbers and attribute them to your efforts and implementation in your life.

That's the Vital 4.

Let recap:

<u>Fitness</u>

.5 point for drinking a green shake.

.5 point for breaking a sweat.

<u>Faith</u>

.5 point for writing down three wins from the day prior.

.5 point for 20 total minutes of meditation.

Family

.5 point each for the message to your significant other and whomever else you choose.

Finances

.5 point for studying something and .5 point for executing it.

That's the entirety of the Vital 4. It's simple and easy to attain. It has to be, or humans won't do it!

I want you to also be thinking about the following as well.

> ## "If you're going to be a high performer with high performing results, you need to have a plan for high performing recovery."

Action Taking Time

Think about this on a daily basis: what are you going to do to keep yourself fresh?

I might take a half-day and get a haircut, then go out and enjoy some delicious food.

It could be cryotherapy.

It could be getting a massage.

It could be a float tank.

It could be a pedicure or manicure.

Whatever it is, you need to do something to back off your tireless work and recover. That's part of success, too, knowing when to take a rest and refuel mentally and physically.

We're always pushing.

If you're a parent and can hear yourself saying, *well, the weekend is where I refresh and get my rest*, then I know for a fact you're not getting the rest and recovery that you need. I know you're spending time doing activities with your family.

That's great, but that's not rest and recovery. You need to be still and let your cells replenish. Let your mind take a break. Let your muscles unclench. That's true rest and recovery.

Find something you can do for yourself to refresh and recharge so that you can be at the top of your game more often than not.

Vital 4 is the foundation.

If you're struggling, let me ask you, are you doing the Vital 4 and not half-assing it? Are you really putting in your all to hit the highest scores possible?

Trust me; when you put the Vital 4 into play, you get results.

The Vital 4 has changed a lot of lives.

It's time to use it to change yours.

Don't look back.

FOCUS, AIM, EXECUTE

CHAPTER 11
CLEARING HURDLES

"Obstacles don't block the path. They are the path." -Zen Proverb

Now I must warn you that once you start implementing the Vital 4 into your life, the obstacles are going to come left and right.

As I mentioned, for me, it was that call from my sister I got at the airport as I was leaving the event—where I learned a lot about what I'm teaching you in this book.

During that call, she informed me of my mom, leaving my dad.

Now, if I'd focused on the negative and thought *poor me, my family is splitting up*; then, I'd probably have returned home and gone right back to my old habits and finding ways to sedate the pain.

But that's not what I did. I had new tools and strategies to help me take on any obstacles thrown at me.

"For the first time, I had control over my thinking. Instead of silencing my inner dialogue, I tapped into it."

That's when it hit me that God had put me at that event for a reason. I couldn't see it before, but I was headed down the same path as my dad. I call that a positive.

My dad showed love by producing in his business and providing for his family. He was my model.

When I started doing what he did, I became successful, but I quickly learned that I wanted more than success.

That event opened my eyes to the possibilities in my life and how I was falling short.

I held success in business as the marker of what success in life is all about. If I wasn't successful in business, then I thought I'd failed in life.

So, when I hit that highest level financially and from a productivity standpoint, and wasn't happy, it scared and excited me at the same time.

I started looking at obstacles as proof that I was headed in the right direction.

Want more proof that the obstacles will be hot on your heels as you level up?

Alright…

My first-weekend event that I hosted for the Gorilla Alliance had six men in attendance.

During the event, I coached them on the Vital 4 amongst other hard-won tools that I was using and am still using in my life.

What I remember is that these men showed a lot of courage and action by taking time from their families to level up. I know it took a lot out of them to be there and to be as focused as they were, and I commend them for it.

It takes a lot to step into the unknown and face your fear of "what if," but what I can tell you is *fear needs to be a green light.*

You need to go deeper into what it is you really fear, and why you are letting it hold you back.

There are lots of lessons and results when you run toward those fears instead of away from them.

We finished up Saturday's all-day event with a nice dinner and then went to bed at the hotel to prepare for another full day.

The next morning, one of the men reached out to let me know that he had to leave early because his stepfather had passed.

There he was, putting in the work, honing his self-awareness to make massive changes in his life that would not only shift his entire existence but those of everyone else around him—and then that obstacle struck!

He wasn't the first to get hit by adversity when trying to improve his life, and he won't be the last.

There are so many stories that I can share with you through the fifteen years I've spent coaching people to level up. If you're not experiencing some type of obstacle, then consider maybe you're not pushing enough.

Life becomes fun when you embrace that life is a problem rolling into another problem—that's how we grow and learn.

Imagine this...

Something negative pops up in your life.

Naturally, our minds want to go to the worst-case scenarios. That's normal. But we can change our instinctual response. We don't have to go there just because we are conditioned to do so.

When we go to the worst-case scenario, it causes us to behave irrationally, which wastes time and energy.

But what if you had filters on your eyes and ears when obstacles pop up?

The filters would help you find a positive when a negative situation appears. All you would be able to see is opportunity within adversity.

If you had that superpower, you could bounce back faster from the hits, which would again save you time and energy.

That filter is what we call Positive Focus, and when you train yourself to find the positive life becomes a life full of lessons.

Positive Focus

Having a Positive Focus means that we can look at a negative situation, and flip it, to find the positive. We can even use that less-than-desirable situation to learn a lesson.

"When you use the Positive Focus every day, it changes how you think."

The next time or two that a negative situation happens, you can look at it, realize what's happening, and then automatically learn a positive lesson from it.

For example, I had a great employee that I loved, trusted, and took very good care of.

He ended up leaving my business and starting his own but decided not to fill me in on his decision until, one day, he left, taking a bunch of clients with him.

I was the last to find out, and when I did, I felt so betrayed and alone.

Why is that a positive?

Well, I can reason that I'm going to save some money and that because he took the action he did, he forced me to make a change that I was scared to make. The incident forced me to react for the better in my business.

When this happened, I decided to take the coaching that I learned from that event and offer it to my clients inside The Vitality Mill.

Doing this excited me and reignited the fire I'd lost for the gym when I'd battled my former franchise.

All because a trainer left and took my clients that I had advertised to get, and who I had signed up myself.

So, what's the lesson?

For new fruit to grow, you have to prune the rotten. AKA, you have to get rid of what's not working and change/shift.

Now, let's apply that lesson to the core Vital 4 areas.

How can you relate that to your Fitness?

Well, if you want to get better results, you have to do things that you haven't done before.

Here are some examples of how I refocused to get the best results out of the critical areas of my life. And how you can do the same.

As it applies to Fitness, maybe I have to eat foods that I haven't tried before. I might have to try new exercises.

When you take these two actions, you are growing and changing by choice. That's a good thing.

That's flipping it.

Do you see how we did that?

As it pertains to my Faith, I might have to change my focus, so I am not fixating on the negative aspects of a situation. When I do that, I can change the way I react to the unexpected.

In Family, if I want to take my marriage to the next level, I have to put in the effort to change-up date nights. They can't be based solely around where my wife and I are going to eat. Because as the saying goes, "For things to change, things must change." Meaning I will keep getting the same results, and my marriage will grow stagnant if I don't put effort into it...that includes date nights.

To take my Finances to another level, I have to monitor what is working and not working when I am trying to bring in new clients. If I'm not changing and shifting, I might find myself losing money.

I may have to save more, cut some costs, or put out new advertising.

Whatever I decide to do, I know something has to change.

Do you see how I just did that?

I turned a negative situation from losing an employee into a positive, learned a lesson from it, and applied that lesson to my Fitness, Faith, Family, and Finances.

You can do this, too, and when you do, use this key to be successful.

- Make sure the lesson learned is simple. Don't make it long and drawn out. When you keep it simple, you can turn it around into a positive quickly so it will better relate to your Vital 4.

Now let me answer a question that might be on your mind.

Why is Positive Focus so important?

Here's the short answer:

> "To get a different result, we need different beliefs. To change our beliefs, we have to change the way we feel. To change how we feel, we have to change how we think."

If you are practicing Positive Focus, you're going to start thinking differently.

But understand, you are not going to hit a home run every time. Change takes consistent effort like anything we do in life. So, keep at it and make it an everyday practice. When a situation occurs that throws you, process it, and then launch into your new Positive Focus way of thinking. You can train yourself to do this over and over again. Just don't stop if it's harder sometimes than others.

The Positive Focus is going to start changing the way you look at things.

But remember, whatever happens, happens.

That's life. We take a positive from it, learn a lesson, and bounce back quickly.

We save time when we do this.

We save energy.

Don't forget…

If we can change the way we think, we can change the way we feel.

If we can change the way we feel, we can change the way we believe.

If we can change the way we believe, we can change our results every single time.

Positive Focus is a game-changer.

I want you to put it into play ASAP in your life.

Do it every single day.

If you are refuting what I am saying with the thought that *I didn't have anything negative happen*, then be assured that Positive Focus can be used in positive situations as well.

Here's an example you can relate to right now.

You finished this chapter.

Why is that a positive?

Because you can now move forward to the next chapter.

As you read the next chapter, I want you to remember the lesson learned: action is the only way to move forward.

Once you have learned this lesson, then relate it back to your Vital 4.

Like this example:

Fitness: Taking action in my fitness will give me better results.

You get the point.

Now let's move on to Chapter 12 and look at our beliefs a bit more deeply to see what we can find.

CHAPTER 12
CHANGE YOUR STORY

"To survive, you must tell stories."
-Umberto Eco

You are the best storyteller alive.

You tell yourself stories every day.

I'm too old.

I'm too fat.

I'm too tired.

I've got too much going on.

I'm overwhelmed.

These stories are enemies to results.

Every morning, thoughts run through your head. They are usually made up of some type of belief.

An example I've used several times from my life is the story concerning my former franchise.

The franchise came after me on a non-compete after opening up The Vitality Mill once I left their franchise.

Let me tell you, running a business while worrying about a lawsuit and secret shoppers is no way to operate.

This took my mind off marketing and sales and focusing on making my business the best it could be. I couldn't be the face of my business under those circumstances.

"This is how I told myself that my story had power."

I told myself *I can't do this. I can't market. I can't advertise. I'm losing it all.*

That's even what I wrote down: "I'm going to lose it all."

Then I took that simple statement and flipped it.

Underneath it, I wrote down the opposite.

"I have it all."

Underneath that, I wrote examples that made that story true.

I have my health

I have a beautiful family.

I have a loving wife.

I have a handsome, athletic, smart son.

I have my mom.

I have my sister, niece, and nephew.

I have my grandma.

I have a custom-built house.

I drive the truck I want.

I own a 10,000 sq. ft. building for my businesses.

That simple act of writing down what I have, became the proof that I *really do* have it all.

The thought of, *I'm going to lose it all* led me to focus on the negative. I told myself *even if they take my business and livelihood; I still have a lot of great people and things in my life*.

Realizing this helped me move forward.

Now once I become aware of the lie that I'm telling myself, when I try to tell it again, I can stop and recognize the lie.

"Awareness precedes change."

Change Your Story Already!

Once you're aware of the junk stories you're telling, you can change your story.

Every single morning, I want you to write down the story that you're telling yourself. This should be a simple, short statement.

It could be:

I'm too old.

I'm too fat.

I'm too tired.

This isn't working, etc.

Whatever you are telling yourself, write that statement down.

Then write down the opposite of that statement.

If you wrote, "I'm too old," your statement will switch to "I'm too young."

It stands to reason then that if you're still young, you can list out all the things you can do that an old person can't do.

When you do this, you build facts around your story. You knock down the negative story you tell yourself.

The new story of self-empowerment helps us take action.

This was, and still is, a game-changer for me. My most successful clients practice it daily.

If we can change the way we think, as I said earlier, we change the way we feel.

Then when we change the way we feel, we change our beliefs.

And by now, you know the rest of this formula: when we change our beliefs, we change our results.

Results change our lives.

Period.

CHAPTER 13

CREATING UNBREAKABLE COMMITMENT

"When you're interested in doing something, you do it only when it's convenient. When you're committed to something, you accept no excuses; only results." -Kenneth Blanchard

By this point, you now have a daily morning routine that you can execute using the Vital 4.

You have a daily practice of using Positive Focus as well as your One Belief—that we'll dive deeper into in a moment.

Now, you need to have a weekly focus.

I've been a part of a lot of transformations, and a mistake I see people make is that they base their results off their emotions.

If they're happy, their results are going to be better that day. If they're sad, mad, or angry, their results won't fare as well.

I base my results and my clients' results off facts.

We want to control what we can control today by hitting our simple targets like breaking a sweat and drinking a green shake.

The majority bounce around from one habit to the other inconsistently and wonder why they don't get a result.

That's why I want you to measure your actual results and not your ideal results.

Once you did that, did you get better results right away?

Quit looking down the road and focus on what is in front of you. That is all that matters; it's mushy but true.

"But how do we stay committed when there is a long road ahead?"

I'm glad you asked.

The Core of Commitment

The human mind is the happiest when it sees progress.

For example, when we know we've done the simple stuff to lose weight—cutting carbs, choosing smaller quantities, etc.—then when we jump on the scale, and it says we haven't dropped weight, it's not going to upset us as much because we did what we were supposed to. So, we can shift our mindset from focusing on what didn't happen to what did.

We can tell ourselves, *you know what? I didn't drop a lot of weight this week, but here are the things I did do.*

By keeping the focus on our wins, we set ourselves up to keep showing up.

Remember: Energy flows where focus goes, and results show.

When we focus on our wins, it means we're always winning.

Then even when we lose, we'll still shift our focus to taking a win from the situation.

Nick Saban, the head football coach at the University of Alabama, was asked about winning championships and what makes Alabama so special. His answer was:

"We're not focused on a championship. We're focused on perfecting the proven process that leads to a championship."

Our process that we're going to focus on will lead to our personal championships. We call these our Key 4.

Inside the Key 4

The Key 4 are the four habits that we need to focus on this week to move us closer to the only thing that matters—aka results.

I want you to take what you're knowingly doing, or not doing, and build four habits around those actions or inactions for the week.

This could be:

"I know I'm not getting enough sleep, so this week I'm going to focus on getting six to eight hours of sleep by going to bed by 9:00 PM every day."

"I know I'm not drinking enough water, so I'm going to drink thirty ounces of water before I have any coffee."

"I know my nutrition is not where it needs to be. So, every day this week, I'm going to log my food into MyFitnessPal to create seven MyFitnessPal entries."

"I need to exercise more, so I'm going to run a mile a day, and that will equal seven miles this week."

Each Sunday, find the four habits that you need to focus on in the coming week to fill the gaps.

To fill a gap from 6-10, what are the four strategies/habits that you need to focus on?

"Write those four things down, and then every morning, remind yourself that you need to do them by putting your attention on your intentions."

Every Sunday, plan ahead as well as look back on your progress. Write out four new habits or keep the habits you used the prior week if they worked for you.

So, if you went to bed on time every night and got eight hours, then you earn one point.

If you plugged all your food into MyFitnessPal, that's another point, and so on.

Each week, score your Key 4 from the previous week, assess how that worked for you, and plan for the week ahead by writing out a fresh Key 4.

When the week starts, that is what you focus on.

That is your only focus.

It's simple.

Persistent.

And consistent.

Regardless of mood, feelings, or emotions, you'll win every time.

CHAPTER 14

FUEL FOR CHANGE

"I am building a fire, and every day I train, I add more fuel. At just the right moment, I light the match." -Mia Hamm

Now let's shift our focus to the Fuel that is running the machine.

Sadly, most people put diesel in a gas engine and wonder why they're not producing the way they want.

Let's be honest—remember what we talked about in the Fact section of the Vital 4? We all know the difference between healthy and unhealthy food.

The problem is that we put restrictions on ourselves.

You're Doing it Wrong

Restrictions force our focus to what *we can't have*.

As I've said in previous chapters, you get what you focus on… So instead of making a long list of what you can't have, start adding in some simple good habits like drinking a green shake daily. Switch the focus of the good you are doing for you.

Doesn't that make more sense?

I've been known to have an addictive personality over the years. To addictions that didn't serve me…

Gambling.

Overeating.

And the list goes on…

In the past, I'd focus on what I shouldn't be doing. I'd waste energy making lists of what I was *not* going to do.

About five years ago, I changed my focus.

Instead of focusing on what I shouldn't be doing…

I focused on becoming addicted to the habits that serve me.

I became obsessed with creating addictions that were productive and gave me what I wanted.

- Green shakes
- Drinking more water
- Working out in the morning
- Showing my family love/appreciation daily
- Meditation
- Finding non-destructive fun
- Cold showers
- Journaling
- Getting my steps in

For years, I focused on what I didn't want but wasn't clear on what I did want. I thought getting rid of what didn't work would get me what I wanted.

The truth that I learned during that time is that simply by shifting your focus, you can become addicted to doing things that create change.

Shift Your Focus, Swap Your Fuel

When I started looking at what I could do right by adding instead of subtracting, the desires for what wasn't working went away.

Since my perspective changed, I wanted a simple nutrition plan to follow. That's exactly why I put together my nutrition manual for the motivated but overwhelmed. I've been in those shoes and know what people need—it's the same solution I needed.

If you need help with nutrition right now, then email me at Seth@TheVitalityMill.com with the subject line: "Nutrition Guide," and I'll send it your way.

"All good nutrition comes down to is asking yourself a question before making a choice."

You need to know: *is this food going to make me feel good now or down the road?*

Food that is terrible for you may taste good now, but that feeling only lasts a few minutes. The negative components of the food are going to set in and start to break down your body. Do this often enough, and your bad food decisions will add up.

In the end, as I have stated, awareness precedes change. Once you're aware of how the food makes you feel, it becomes easier to make a long-term change.

And...it always helps to remember this when you are trying to better your nutrition: If you feel like crap, you'll perform like crap.

Besides, you'll *never* outperform the way you feel.

CHAPTER 15

MOTIVATION MEANS ACTION

"The past is your lesson. The present is your gift. The future is your motivation." -Unknown

So, I believe I've made it pretty clear that you're in control of how you feel, but you're also in control of your behaviors.

Everything we do with The Vital 4 benefits one or both of the above. The same holds true for Positive Focus and executing One Belief at a Time.

Most people will say they're not motivated or that they don't have the time, and that's why they don't work out.

When in actuality, we all have the same amount of time in the day, and some of the busiest successful individuals I know still somehow find the time to break a sweat.

I'll have you consider we don't have a time or motivation problem; we have an energy problem.

Now don't get it twisted. Motivation has a role in encouraging us to take action, but it will run out at some point. So we don't want to depend on it, but we can always increase our energy.

Let's say your energy is a little low today, and you need a bump of motivation to get you going.

Then we need to know how can we add a shot of motivation to your body to energize you enough to work out? How can we do this right from the jump?

Making Motivation

Some people give themselves a jolt of high-energy music when they work out, and that gets them charged up. But you can't always turn on your favorite music.

Personally, I want to create motivation as fast as I can and as easily as possible.

And you might think this is weird, but I believe the best way to create motivation is through powerful questions. I learned this from one of my coaches, Paul Mort.

Some examples to ask yourself first thing in the morning are...

- What do I have to look forward to today?
- Who needs me on my A-game today?
- Who would benefit from me having more confidence and energy?

By asking ourselves powerful questions, it gives us the motivation to take action.

If I'm shifting my focus to what I have to look forward to for the day, then I'm not focusing on all that I have to do.

If I ask myself a question, "Like who needs me to show up for them today?" I think about my wife, son, mom, and clients. It reminds me that others depend on me, which inspires me to do the work.

Your Vital 4 Morning Routine & Motivation

By asking ourselves powerful questions in the morning, the motivation we need to take our first step of action is generated. Then once we take that first step, we create the momentum to keep us pushing forward.

We want to resist the urge to overthink in the morning. That is why we need to have our Vital 4 morning routine laid out and ready to put into play without having to think about it. It saves us time and energy.

I don't know about you, but the morning is usually when I feel anxious and overwhelmed. When I use the Vital 4, my focus shifts from how I feel to what I need to accomplish; it just so happens the items I need to accomplish are increasing my energy and focus—and that sets me up to win the morning. I know if I can win the morning, I have an improved probability of winning the day.

Now that we're clear on how important energy is and that motivation is a part of it—but like willpower, it will run out—we can look at one more way to push ourselves forward.

Data Moves You Along

Data holds a key to how hard we push ourselves. Here's a fun fact. Did you know...

"Your mind is happiest when it's making progress?"

We need data to show us we're improving.
Not to mention, working out can get boring for some people.

When we're not working toward something, we get comfortable, and that can be a slippery slope. Late-night pantry hunting gets me, but if I have a goal that I'm working toward and have created leverage via accountability, then I'll be more likely to stay away from the pantry.

In my 30-Day Program, The Momentum Activator, I prescribe my clients to reach a mile as fast as possible or to log 10,000 steps as soon as they possibly can. Both of these goals gives them something to work toward and track while also providing a simple way to break a sweat. Let me make something very clear. Some of us do not need hard, crazy workouts. If your sleep and recovery are horrible, then that's where we need to start instead of a hard workout.

How do I know the tracking of a mile works?

Meet Nate

I tested data on my college and frat brother, Nate Nelson. Nate is an outgoing successful DJ with a beautiful wife and two kids. I was watching Nate on Facebook like the majority of us do, and I noticed from the outside that Nate had it all except one thing.

Nate needed to drop about 150lbs., so one day, I hit him up and asked him to join me for ninety days. He thought about it and then declined.

He did what a majority do and talked himself out of taking action. I have to be honest, it kind of pissed me off, so I went back to the drawing board. Then I created the 30-Day Momentum Activator, and since it was less of a commitment, I went back to Nate.

Nate turned me down again. A couple of days later, he went and took his nine-year-old daughter, Mollie, to ride roller coasters at Six Flags. They waited in line for one ride for ninety minutes. Then when it was finally their turn, and they went to get in the car, Nate didn't fit in the seat.

He was embarrassed, but a lady, who was riding by herself, offered to ride with Mollie. And Mollie wanted to ride badly, so Nate let her go.

Nate felt horrible missing out on the experience with Mollie. When the ride ended, the lady let Nate know that Mollie had hit her head pretty hard while riding and that he might want to keep an eye on her. Then Nate felt extra horrible because he'd put his daughter at risk.

The next day I received a text from Nate that he was ready to get after it.

I didn't give him anything but the same simple tactics I'm teaching you in this book. Nutrition-wise, I gave him the exact nutrition guide I'm offering you—if you email me at Seth@TheVitalityMill.com with the subject line "Nutrition Guide."

Nate started walking every morning and then running. In less than a year, Nate was down 135 lbs.

It all started with hitting The Vital 4 every morning.

Then he'd record the time he'd taken to run a mile and share it with me.

So Nate had a proven plan to follow, but he also had leverage because he never wanted to put his family at risk again. Six months after working with me, Nate took Mollie back to Six Flags, and they rode that ride together.

*****

When we hit the pavement the first thing in the morning, already we're working toward something, so we're happy; we already have motivation, but we're also creating more momentum by keeping it simple.

If you're just starting out, that's a great formula for success. The only place you have to go is up. You have no choice but to create motivation, and you can coast on that for a little while as short-term motivation infusion.

Now, let's implement that into our lives to progress them long-term.

We'll use Nate as our example.

Nate created his leverage because of his incident with Mollie and putting her at risk. That moment gave him the drive to do the simple mile and the Vital 4.

But what if you don't have that type of leverage like Nate?

"How can you create more leverage to force yourself to do the work?"

For my clients and me, that means living a challenge-based lifestyle. And there are all sorts of ways you can do this!

Live a Challenge-Based Lifestyle

You might book a 5K, half marathon, CrossFit competition, or mud race—if you want to live a challenge-based lifestyle.

The booking part of your plan is critical because when you register for an event, you've set yourself up for accountability for the next ninety days. You have to do the work, and if you don't, you won't like the alternative. No one wants to show up to an event unprepared and embarrassed.

That's what I mean by stating that a challenge-based lifestyle gives you leverage.

When I started living a challenge-based lifestyle, I was working with a group of other men who owned gyms.

We would meet up every ninety days and set 90-day targets. This gave us leverage because no one wants to be the guy or gal in the group who doesn't do what he or she said they would.

One day, this group of guys and I were sitting in San Diego. I was stuck on what I wanted to do for my 90-day target. Some guys were setting boxing matches; others were climbing mountains. One guy suggested, "Seth, there is a CrossFit event close to you in April," and that was that.

I booked the event and started training.

To create additional leverage, I also got on Facebook and told everyone that not only was I going to participate, but I was going to win.

This gave me leverage, like no other target I had set in the past.

I got in the best shape of my life during those ninety days. Everything was rocking and rolling until Super Bowl Sunday when my son and I headed out to play a pick-up game of one-on-one basketball.

He was at the stage where I had to put in effort, or he'd beat me...and that just can't happen.

I went up to block his shot and then jumped back up to grab the ball after I tipped it. When I came down hard on his large foot, I knew I had injured myself immediately.

My mind sped ahead to my event, and I panicked for a minute. I found out shortly after a trip to the doctor that I had torn the ligaments in my ankle. As soon as I heard the news, I told myself there was no way I was going to quit.

Here I was leveling up my fitness and feeling great, and then the obstacles arrived. So, I devised a plan and worked around my ankle. I focused on getting it healed through chiropractor visits, cryotherapy, and...you name it, I tried it. My ankle lacked mobility, but I went to the event anyway.

After spending all day on my ankle, it was pretty screwed up, but I still had a great day and made it to the finals.

I remember being worried about my ankle and walking over to find out what the final event had in store for me.

The first exercise was box jumps, which was something I hadn't tried since hurting my ankle.

I was apprehensive at first but gave it the best I could and ended up getting third in the final competition.

After the competition, I was super frustrated with my third-place showing until I learned the finals were just a piece of the score.

Once they totaled all the events, I won first place!

This challenge was a game-changer for me in a few ways.

I fought through an injury and won the event, which took my confidence to another level.

It kept me focused on a goal to work toward, which I believe we all need.

I proved to myself that I show up and do what I say, regardless of the circumstances.

That's one way to leverage yourself in your Fitness area.

Another way to leverage yourself to win in your Fitness is to set a processed-based goal.

The way this works is that you set up certain times to accomplish something in a certain amount of days.

For example, it may be…

"I'm going to run thirty miles in thirty days."

"I'm going to work out with my trainer sixteen times in thirty days."

You could also have an event-based goal setup with a process-based goal…

That might look like…

"I have a 5K in ninety days (event), and each day I'm going to run a mile (process) at the end of the week. So, if I run seven miles, I know I'm on track."

You can even take this up a notch by going online and telling everyone about your 5K.

Last but not least, another way to create leverage is by putting out what you plan to accomplish in public and telling your kids, too.

"No one wants to be the guy who doesn't back up what they say, especially to their kids—who look to us as role models."

So, to recap...

- Get clear on what you want.
- Set a target by creating leverage either through an event, process-based goal, or a public declaration.
- Every morning create motivation by asking yourself tough questions.
- Keep the momentum going by falling into your morning routine with the Vital 4.

CHAPTER 16
PERFORMANCE IN PLAY

"By their fruits, you will know them." -Jesus Christ.

<u>Results don't lie.</u>

And in my humble and 100-percent accurate opinion, results are not hard to come by when you have a plan, leverage, consistency and accountability.

The problem is that we're not clear on the result we want most of the time.

As you know by now, if we're not sure about the result, it's impossible to create a sustainable plan to get to where we want to go without wasting time, money, and energy.

Now, I know I've laid a lot on you, and the last thing I want is for you to go into information overload.

In this next chapter, I'm going to go over a quick overview, so we're clear to move forward.

Overview

Start with getting down to the facts of where you are right now. This is where you'll rate yourself from a 1-10, and then you'll figure out how you can fill the gap between your number and 10 with actionable steps to move yourself forward.

Once you're clear on where you're beginning, you can then look at habits you may need to drop.

Then ask yourself a powerful question that will cut through all the BS.

> ## *"What are you knowingly doing that is stopping you from the results you want?"*

Once you answer that question, you'll see the obstacles that you need to work through. Write down these obstacles and keep them for when you start to build out your 90-day targets.

Now you have a pretty good idea of where you need to level up so you can build your 90-day Vital 4 Targets.

For each of The Vital 4 areas, you will build a clear 90-day target.

Break down the questions that can be asked in the Vital 4 areas here:

- What's the 90-day outcome and the deadline?
- What's the 60-day benchmark and the date you'll check in?
- What's the 30-day benchmark and the date you'll check in?
- Why does the 90-day outcome matter to you? (What's the payoff/benefit/leverage?)
- How will you create accountability and/or urgency?
- What are the three biggest obstacles you'll face trying to reach this outcome?
- How will you specifically overcome these obstacles, and when will you overcome them?

You want to take the time and answer these questions because if you lack clarity on what's required, you'll also lack the motivation to do what's required.

If you're not sure what's required, then take out a piece of paper.

On one side of the paper, write down every obstacle you can possibly think of that will stop you from hitting your goal.

On the other side of the paper, write down a strategy you can use to overcome each obstacle.

The strategies will become your Key 4, aka your game plan for the week.

Now that you have targets to work toward and obstacles to overcome them, you can focus on your Key 4 daily.

I'd suggest waking up every day and reminding yourself of your intentions for the day, including in your Vital 4 morning routine foundation. Remember the Vital 4 is non-negotiable. You use it to live a high-performance life, so you need to make sure you carve out this time to accomplish it in your schedule daily.

In my calendar, I schedule myself first because if I don't take care of me, then I can't show up for others on the level they deserve.

After I schedule myself in the calendar, I then schedule any family events like my son's games, date nights, etc.

Next, I schedule in my work.

Most people tell me they don't have time for what they need to do until I ask them for their calendar. Then it's a different story. Be relentless with your time and make it count.

As we know, the obstacles will come hot and heavy at you, and that's why it's vital that you lean on the Positive Focus daily. It will shift your focus out of the negative, and over time, it'll become a reaction.

The same goes for One Belief at a Time. You need to take inventory of the stories you're telling yourself daily, which will lead to an awareness of the stories that are holding you back.

One of those stories I told myself was that there was no way I could write a book. But here we are—wrapping up the last chapter.

> "If there is one thing I hope you take from this book, it's that we're all the same. We all struggle. We all want to be the best we can be, and if we're pushing, we're going to have setbacks. That's how we learn."

I don't know where you're in your life right now but keep pushing forward daily regardless of your mood, feelings and emotions. Every day won't be your best, but you can always give it your best. I pray this book gives you a framework.

I'm super grateful and humbled that you took the time to read my book. If you'd be interested in working with me for thirty days where I'll coach you to create the energy you need and hold you accountable to take on everything in this book and more, all you have to do is go to:

www.MomentumActivator.com.

I'll reach out and guide you from there. If you have any questions, don't hesitate to reach out to me at Seth@TheGorillaAlliance.com.

ACKNOWLEDGMENTS

Courtney- You have stuck by me through thick and thin. In my darkest times, you've been my light. You're the dream partner in this game of life. I love you more than you can ever imagine and will never forget all you've done for my family and me.

Colt- You and your mom were the best things that happened to me. I'm so damn proud of you, and I'm excited to see the impact that you make. I couldn't have picked a better son, and I'm so grateful every time I hear you call me "Pops." Love you, boy!

Mom-Thank you for always pushing me to better, for seeing in me what I couldn't see. I appreciate all that you did for our family and all the skills you passed down to me. I love you more!

Mimi- My biggest fan, I've been in the wrong so many times, but you always found the good in me. Thank you for being my protector when I shouldn't have been protected. I love you, and I'm forever grateful to call you my Mimi.

ABOUT THE AUTHOR

Seth Humphrey is the founder and CEO of The Vitality Mill, StretchU & The Gorilla Alliance,

His businesses were created to help each client unlock their most elite version of themselves.

Seth is married to his college sweetheart and has an eighteen-year-old son who plays college football at The University of Houston.

BONUS!

Kick start your momentum today. Head over to momentumactivator.com and I'll reach out and guide you from there. If you have any questions, don't hesitate to reach out to me at Seth@TheGorillaAlliance.com